TREASURY OF LITERATURE
READ-ALOUD ANTHOLOGY

HARCOURT BRACE & COMPANY
Orlando   Atlanta   Austin   Boston   San Francisco   Chicago   Dallas   New York
Toronto   London

Black Butterfly Children's Books: "Making Friends" from *Nathaniel Talking* by Eloise Greenfield, illustrated by Jan Spivey Gilchrist. Text copyright © 1988 by Eloise Greenfield; illustrations copyright © 1988 by Jan Spivey Gilchrist.
Ruth Cohen, Inc., on behalf of Patrick J. Gallagher, Executor: Chicken Forgets by Miska Miles. Text copyright © 1976 by Miska Miles. Published by Little, Brown and Company.
Lois Lenski Covey Foundation Inc.: "Winter Cold" from *City Poems* by Lois Lenski. Text copyright 1954, 1965 by Lois Lenski; text copyright © 1956, 1971 by Lois Lenski.
C. P. P./Belwin, Inc., Miami, FL 33014: Music from "Ten Little Frogs" (Retitled: "Five Little Frogs") by Lucille F. Wood and Louise B. Scott. Copyright © 1954 by Bowmar Noble; copyright renewed by Bowmar Noble and assigned to Belwin-Mills Publishing Corp. All rights reserved.
Crown Publishers, Inc.: Mother, Mother, I Want Another by Maria Polushkin, illustrated by Diane Dawson. Text copyright © 1978 by Maria Polushkin; illustrations copyright © 1978 by Diane Dawson.
Dial Books for Young Readers, a division of Penguin Books USA Inc.: "Summer Vacation" from *My Daddy Is a Cool Dude and Other Poems* by Karama Fufuka. Text copyright © 1975 by Karama Fufuka.
Doubleday, a division of Bantam Doubleday Dell Publishing Group, Inc.: Angus and the Cat by Marjorie Flack. Text copyright 1931 by Marjorie Flack Larsson.
Dover Publications, Inc.: Music and lyrics from "The Allee-Allee O" in *Singing Games and Playparty Games* by Richard Chase.
Folkways Music Publishers, Inc., New York: Music and lyrics from "Riding in My Car" by Woody Guthrie. Copyright © 1954 by TRO, renewed 1969 by Folkways Music Publishers, Inc.
Greenwillow Books, a division of William Morrow & Company, Inc.: "Frog's Lullaby" from *All Asleep* by Charlotte Pomerantz. Text copyright © 1984 by Charlotte Pomerantz.
Harcourt Brace Jovanovich, Inc.: "My Father" and "My Mother" from *Everything Glistens and Everything Sings* by Charlotte Zolotow. Text copyright © 1987 by Charlotte Zolotow. "A Gift," "The Days of the Week," and "In the Clear Water" from *BRIGHT START: A Pocketful of Poems.* Text copyright © 1991 by Harcourt Brace Jovanovich, Inc.
HarperCollins Publishers: The Seashore Noisy Book by Margaret Wise Brown. Text copyright © 1941 by Margaret Wise Brown. "Cats Sleep Anywhere" from *The Children's Bells* by Eleanor Farjeon. Text copyright © by The Estate of Eleanor Farjeon. Published by Oxford University Press. "The Furry Ones" from *Feathered Ones and Furry* by Aileen Fisher. Text copyright © 1971 by Aileen Fisher. *The Baby Beebee Bird* by Diane Redfield Massie. Text copyright © 1963 by Diane Redfield Massie. "Little Seeds" from *The Winds That Come from Far Away* by Else Holmelund Minarik, illustrated by Joan Phyllis Berg. Text copyright © 1964 by Else Holmelund Minarik; illustrations copyright © 1964 by Joan Phyllis Berg. "The Lion and the Mouse," "The Three Bears," and "The Gingerbread Man" from *The Three Bears & 15 Other Stories* by Anne Rockwell. Text copyright © 1975 by Anne Rockwell.
Harvard University Press, Cambridge, MA: Music and lyrics from "Who's That Tapping at the Window?" in *On the Trail of Negro Folk Songs* by Dorothy Scarborough. Copyright © 1925 by Harvard University Press, 1953 by Mary McDaniel Parker.
High/Scope Press, Ypsilanti, MI: Music and lyrics from "Barnacle Bill" in *Movement Plus Rhymes, Songs, & Singing Games* by Phyllis S. Weikart. Published by High/Scope Press, 1988.
William I. Kaufman: "Challenge of the Sun and the Wind" from *UNICEF Book of Children's Legends* by William I. Kaufman. Text copyright © 1970 by William I. Kaufman.
Kids Can Press Ltd., Toronto, Canada: Franklin in the Dark by Paulette Bourgeois, illustrated by Brenda Clark. Text copyright © 1986 by Paulette Bourgeois; illustrations copyright © 1986 by Brenda Clark.
Little, Brown and Company: "Bananas and Cream" from *One at a Time* by David McCord. Text copyright © 1961, 1962 by David McCord. "Song of the Train" from *One at a Time* by David McCord. Text copyright 1952 by David McCord.
Lothrop, Lee & Shepard Books, a division of William Morrow & Company, Inc.: Music from "The Mulberry Bush," "Bingo," "The Bear Went Over the Mountain," "The Muffin Man," and "Did You Ever See a Lassie?" in *SINGING BEE! A Collection of Favorite Children's Songs,* compiled by Jane Hart. Copyright © 1982 by Jane Hart.
Ludlow Music, Inc., New York: Music and lyrics from "Mary Wore Her Red Dress" ("Mary Was a Red Bird") and "The Wind Blow East," collected, adapted, and arranged by John A. Lomax and Alan Lomax. Copyright © 1941 by TRO, renewed by Ludlow Music, Inc.
Gina Maccoby Literary Agency: "Giraffes" from *The Raucous Auk* by Mary Ann Hoberman. Text copyright © 1973 by Mary Ann Hoberman. Published by Viking Penguin. "Night" from *Hello and Good-By* by Mary Ann Hoberman. Text copyright © 1959, renewed 1987 by Mary Ann Hoberman. Published by Little, Brown and Company.
Macmillan Publishing Company: "The Little Turtle" from *Collected Poems of Vachel Lindsay.* Text copyright 1920 by Macmillan Publishing Company, renewed 1948 by Elizabeth C. Lindsay. *Will I Have a Friend?* by Miriam Cohen, illustrated by Lillian Hoban. Text copyright © 1967 by Miriam Cohen; illustrations copyright © 1967 by Lillian Hoban.
Mariposa Printing & Publishing Inc.: "Coyote & Turtle" from *Coyote & . . .: Native American Folk Tales,* retold by Joe Hayes. Text copyright © 1983 by Joe Hayes.
McClelland and Stewart Ltd., Toronto: Music and lyrics from "Roll Over" in *Sally Go Round the Sun* by Edith Fowke. Copyright © 1969 by McClelland and Stewart Ltd.
Margaret K. McElderry Books, an imprint of Macmillan Publishing Company: "Invitation" from *There Was a Place and Other Poems* by Myra Cohn Livingston. Text copyright © 1988 by Myra Cohn Livingston.
Marci Ridlon McGill: "Hamsters" from *That Was Summer* by Marci Ridlon. Text copyright © 1969 by Marci Ridlon. Published by Follett Publishing Co., 1969.
Orchard Books, New York: Mr. Floop's Lunch by Matt Novak. Copyright © 1990 by Matt Novak.
Anita E. Posey: "When All the World's Asleep" by Anita E. Posey from *Rings and Things.* Published by Macmillan Publishing Company, 1967.
Marian Reiner, on behalf of Myra Cohn Livingston: "Clay" from *A Song I Sang to You* by Myra Cohn Livingston. Text copyright © 1984, 1969, 1967, 1965, 1959, 1958 by Myra Cohn Livingston.
Marian Reiner, on behalf of Beatrice Schenk de Regniers: "Keep a Poem in Your Pocket" from *Something Special* by Beatrice Schenk de Regniers. Text copyright © 1958 by Beatrice Schenk de Regniers, renewed © 1986.
Sidney Robertson, collector: "Bought Me a Cat."
Scholastic Inc.: "Zip, Zap, Zoom" from *Scholastic Early Childhood Program, Language and Reading Teaching Guide.* Text copyright © 1981 by Scholastic, Inc.
Charles Scribner's Sons, an imprint of Macmillan Publishing Company: "If You Ever" and "Five Little Chickens" (Retitled: "The Chickens") from *The Poetry Troupe,* compiled by Isabel Wilner. Published by Charles Scribner's Sons, 1977.
Silver Burdett & Ginn, Inc.: Lyrics from "What Shall We Do?" in *World of Music* by Mary Palmer, Mary Louise Reilly, and Carol Rogel Scott. ©1966, 1971, 1988 by Silver Burdett & Ginn Inc.
The Society of Authors, on behalf of the Estate of Rose Fyleman: "The Chickens" by Rose Fyleman.
Songs Music, Inc.: Music and lyrics from "The Bus Song" (Retitled: "The Wheels on the Bus") in *Eye Winker Tom Tinker Chin Chopper: Fifty Musical Fingerplays* by Tom Glazer. © by Songs Music, Inc. Published by Doubleday.
Warren-Mattox Productions: Music and lyrics from "Little Sally Walker" and "Loop de Loo" in *Shake It to the One That You Love the Best,* adapted by Cheryl Warren Mattox. Copyright © 1989 by Warren-Mattox Productions.
Western Publishing Company, Inc.: "Dig a Little Hole" from *Little Boy Blue: Fingerplays Old and New* by Daphne Hogstrom. Text © 1966 by Western Publishing Company, Inc.

POEMS and RHYMES

Reading Aloud to Children

by Dr. Dorothy S. Strickland

Read to your children daily! Read with enthusiasm! Read in a manner that stimulates reflection, talk, and interaction.

Reading aloud to children is a part of every teacher's repertoire of "absolute musts." Its value is passed along to parents as one of the few universal truths in education.

Reading aloud builds background knowledge. Poems like "Little Seeds" and "Song of the Train" can trigger conversations about how things grow, or reflections on a memorable trip. Reading that is linked with real-life events enhances both the real and the vicarious experiences.

Sharing literature with children increases their vocabulary and their awareness of sentence structure and of the sounds of language. Poems and stories are full of interesting ways to describe, to compare, and to contrast: "the little wee bear," "the great big bear." Children unconsciously incorporate these models into their own thoughts and speech.

Exposing listeners to sentence structures outside of ordinary speech— "Twinkle, twinkle, little star/How I wonder what you are"—is another service that literature performs uniquely well. Giving children opportunities to play with the sounds of language through the rhyme and rhythm of poetry is yet another.

Exposure to a variety of literary forms provides the listener with knowledge that he or she needs to understand literature. Fables, such as "The Lion and the Mouse," and story elements, such as the contrast between good and evil portrayed in "The Three Billy-Goats Gruff," are basic literary components that children will meet over and over again throughout life. This knowledge is called upon by children as they write stories and poems and as they discuss the writing of others. Thus, reading aloud promotes reading-writing relationships, a key factor in children's literacy development. The benefits from reading aloud to children are deep and abiding. Lucky is the child with whom it is done frequently and well.

Techniques for Reading Aloud to Children

by Ellen Booth Church

The selections included in this anthology can be read aloud, sung, recited, or acted out. Even though there is a variety of ways to approach these selections, there are some basic techniques to keep in mind.

Include a visual. Being visually oriented, kindergartners are more attentive when there is something for them to see. Consider the literature, and decide what would best serve to capture children's interest. Short poems, rhymes, and songs make great charts that can later be illustrated by the children. Writing the verse on the board offers a different approach. A stuffed animal, a puppet, a related prop, or good facial expressions and hand motions can give children the visual focus that they need.

Organize the group. Take time to get everyone seated comfortably in a place where he or she can see. The event can be lost if children are not paying attention from the beginning of the activity. Whisper, sing a song, sit quietly, or do whatever seems necessary to create an ambience with the group.

Engage children's interest and excitement during the first reading of the selection. Usually, you'll want children to hear the selection as a whole before examining it. They love to help you read by joining in on repeated readings.

Read dramatically. Use different voices and inflections to represent the characters and the events of the piece. Pause in appropriate places to emphasize a point or to regain children's attention. Slow down or speed up as the text indicates. When reading poems and other rhyming pieces, accent the rhyming words, eventually leaving out a rhyming word for the children to fill in.

Invite children to participate in the reading. Children can tap quietly, clap rhythmically, or perform hand motions in the background as the selection is being read. Most of all, children enjoy saying the selection with you. So read slowly and with expression. Whatever techniques you choose, remember that all of these methods are designed to make the selection come alive for the listener.

Keep
a Poem
in Your
Pocket

Keep a poem in your pocket
and a picture in your head
and you'll never feel lonely
at night when you're in bed.

The little poem will sing to you
the little picture bring to you
a dozen dreams to dance to you
at night when you're in bed.

So —
Keep a picture in your pocket
and a poem in your head
and you'll never feel lonely
at night when you're in bed.

Beatrice Schenk de Regniers

Diddle, Diddle, Dumpling

Diddle, diddle, dumpling, my son John
Went to bed with his trousers on;
One shoe off, and one shoe on,
Diddle, diddle, dumpling, my son John.

Jack and Jill

Jack and Jill
Went up the hill
To fetch a pail of water;
Jack fell down
And broke his crown,
And Jill came tumbling after.

Hickory, Dickory, Dock!

Hickory, dickory, dock!
The mouse ran up the clock;
The clock struck one
And down he run.
Hickory, dickory, dock!

Little Miss Muffet

Little Miss Muffet
Sat on her tuffet,
Eating her curds and whey;
There came a big spider,
Who sat down beside her
And frightened Miss Muffet away.

Little Jack Horner

Little Jack Horner
Sat in the corner,
Eating his Christmas pie;
He put in his thumb,
And pulled out a plum,
And said, What a good boy am I!

One Misty, Moisty Morning

One misty, moisty morning
When cloudy was the weather,
I chanced to meet an old man
Clothed all in leather.

He began to compliment,
And I began to grin.
How do you do? And how do you do,
And how do you do again?

Three Little Kittens

Three little kittens…they lost their mittens,

  And they began to cry,

Oh, Mother dear, we sadly fear

  Our mittens we have lost.

What! lost your mittens,

  You naughty kittens!

Then you shall have no pie.

  Mee-ow, mee-ow, mee-ow.

No, you shall have no pie.

The three little kittens…they found their mittens,

  And they began to cry,

Oh! Mother dear, see here, see here,

  Our mittens we have found.

Put on your mittens,

  You silly kittens,

And you shall have some pie.

  Purr-r, purr-r, purr-r.

Oh, let us have some pie.

The three little kittens put on their mittens
And soon ate up the pie;
Oh, Mother dear, we greatly fear
Our mittens we have soiled.
What! soiled your mittens,
You naughty kittens!
Then they began to sigh,
Mee-ow, mee-ow, mee-ow,
Then they began to sigh.

The three little kittens… they washed their mittens
And hung them out to dry;
Oh, Mother dear, do you not hear,
Our mittens we have washed.
What! washed your mittens,
Then you're good kittens,
But I smell a rat close by,
Mee-ow, mee-ow, mee-ow,
We smell a rat close by.

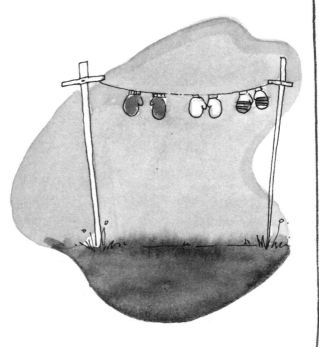

Summer Vacation

We read books in school
and we write stories
about what we did on
summer vacation.

This summer,
I played ball
and went to the beach
and Mama brought home
a brand-new baby.

Karama Fufuka

The Days of the Week

Monday and Tuesday
Are two, you see.
Monday and Tuesday and Wednesday, three.
Thursday and Friday are five.
Thursday and Friday and Saturday, six.
Sunday seven.

Los dias de la semana

Lunes y martes
son dos, como ves.
Lunes y martes y miercoles, tres.
Jueves y viernes son cinco, vereis.
Jueves y viernes y sabado, seis.
Domingo siete.

Clay

Oh, so many things to make.
A dog and a basket, a cat and a snake:
I'm rolling,
I'm pushing,
I'm squeezing,
I'm squishing,
I'm poking,
I'm pinching,
I'm twisting,
I'm wishing,
a piece of clay into a ring,
a face
a flower—
everything!

Myra Cohn Livingston

My Mother

My mother is soft

with a pillow smell

powdery and warm.

She is like a fragrant tree

holding out her arms to me.

Charlotte Zolotow

My Father

My father is tall

and strong as a giant.

I bet

with his bare hands

he could break rocks in half.

But when I told him this one day,

he picked me up

and held me close

so that I *felt* his tenderness and

the rumble of his laugh.

Charlotte Zolotow

Invitation

Listen! I've a big surprise!
My new mom has light-green eyes

and my new brother, almost ten,
is really smart. He helped me when

we did our homework. They moved in
a week ago. When we begin

to settle down, she said that you
could come for dinner. When you do

you'll like them, just like Dad and me,
so come and meet my family!

Myra Cohn Livingston

A Gift

To you, my mother,
I come to offer this
A beautiful bouquet
Which I've just made.

Every single flower
Comes to say
Just how much I love you,
And to wish you happiness.

traditional

Regalo

A ti, madre mia,
te vengo a ofrecer
este lindo ramo
que acabo de hacer.

Cada florecita
te viene a decir
que te quiero mucho
y que seas feliz.

tradicional

Bananas and Cream

Bananas and cream,
Bananas and cream:
All we could say was
Bananas and cream.

We couldn't say fruit,
We wouldn't say cow,
We didn't say sugar—
We don't say it now.

Bananas and cream,
Bananas and cream,
All we could shout was
Bananas and cream.

We didn't say why,
We didn't say how;
We forgot it was fruit,
We forgot the old cow;
We *never* said sugar,
We only said WOW!

Bananas and cream,
Bananas and cream;
All that we want is
Bananas and cream!

We didn't say dish,
We didn't say spoon;
We said not tomorrow,
But NOW and HOW SOON

Bananas and cream,
Bananas and cream?
We yelled for bananas,
Bananas and scream!

David McCord

Making Friends

when I was in kindergarten

this new girl came in our class one day

and the teacher told her to sit beside me

and I didn't know what to say

so I wiggled my nose and made my bunny face

and she laughed

then she puffed out her cheeks

and she made a funny face

and I laughed

so then

we were friends

Eloise Greenfield

Cats Sleep Anywhere

Cats sleep
Anywhere,
Any table,
Any chair,
Top of piano,
Window-ledge,
In the middle,
On the edge,
Open drawer,
Empty shoe,
Anybody's
Lap will do,
Fitted in a
Cardboard box,
In the cupboard
With your frocks —
Anywhere!
They don't care!
Cats sleep
Anywhere.

Eleanor Farjeon

Hamsters

Hamsters are the nicest things
That anyone could own.
I like them even better than
Some dogs that I have known.

Their fur is soft, their faces nice.
They're small when they are grown.
And they sit inside your pocket
When you are all alone.

Marci Ridlon

The Furry Ones

I like —
the furry ones —
the waggy ones
the hoppy ones
the purry ones
that hurry,

The glossy ones
the saucy ones
the sleepy ones
the leapy ones
the mousy ones
that scurry,

The snuggly ones
the huggly ones
the never, never
ugly ones…
all soft
and warm
and furry.

Aileen Fisher

Giraffes

Giraffes
  I like them.
  Ask me why.
    Because they hold their heads up high.
    Because their necks stretch to the sky.
    Because they're quiet, calm, and shy.
    Because they run so fast they fly,
    Because their eyes are velvet brown.
    Because their coats are spotted tan.
    Because they eat the tops of trees.
    Because their legs have knobby knees.
    Because
    Because
    Because. That's why
  I like giraffes.

Mary Ann Hoberman

Zip, Zap, Zoom

Did you see that zebra go zipping by?
    Zip, zap, zoom!
He's going to the zoo with a cherry pie.
    Zip, zap, zoom!
It's Zelda the elephant's fifth birthday.
    Zip, zap, zoom!
Go, zebra, go! The pie's getting away!
    Zip, zap, zoom!

The Lion Hunt

TEACHER: We're going on a Lion Hunt.
CHILDREN: *We're going on a Lion Hunt.*
TEACHER: All righty?
CHILDREN: *All righty.*
TEACHER: Let's go!
CHILDREN: *Let's go!*

(Pattern continues throughout)

Oh, look!
What's that?
It's a bridge.
We can't go around it.
We can't go under it.
We have to go over it.
All righty?
Let's go!
(*Make a thumping noise
on chests with fists.*)

(Refrain)

Oh, look!
What's that?
It's some grass.
We can't go around it.
We can't go under it.
We have to go through it.
All righty?
Let's go!
(*Make swooshing sounds with hands.*)

(Refrain)

21

Oh, look!
What's that?
It's some mud.
We can't go around it.
We can't go under it.
We have to go through it.
All righty?
Let's go!
(*Make mushing sounds with hands.*)

(Refrain)

Oh, look!
What's that?
It's a tree!
We can't go under it.
We can't go over it.
We have to climb up it!
All righty?
Let's go!
(*Make climbing motions and sounds.*)

(Refrain)

Oh, LOOK!!!!
WHAT'S THAT?????
IT'S A **LION**!!
LET'S GO!!

Down the tree! (*climbing motions*)
Through the mud! (*mud sounds and motions*)
Through the grass! (*grass sounds and motions*)
Over the bridge! (*bridge sounds*)
Run home! (*motions with arms*)
Slam the door! (*door closing motion with a clap sound*)
WHEW, we made it! (*wiping brow*)
We weren't afraid,
Were we?
No, not us!

Winter Cold

Snow is so deep
    and wet and cold,
Keeps coming down
    fold on fold;
Covers the walks
    and the railroad tracks,
Blows great drifts up
    front and back.

Men with a shovel
    pile it high,
Beside the sidewalk
    where people go by;
Cars get stalled,
    trucks break down,
Too much snow
    in this little old town!

Go get your jacket,
Your rubber boots too;
Zip up your zipper —
Whatever you do.
Let's go out wading,
Make snowballs and throw;
Nothing more fun
Than to play in the snow!

Lois Lenski

23

Song of the Train

Clickety-clack,
Wheels on the track,
This is the way
They begin the attack:
Click-ety-clack,
Click-ety-clack,
Click-ety, *clack-ety*,
Click-ety
Clack.

Clickety-clack,
Over the crack,
Faster and faster
The song of the track:
Clickety-clack,
Clickety-clack,
Clickety, clackety
Clackety
Clack.

Riding in front,
Riding in back,
Everyone hears
The song of the track:
Clickety-clack,
Clickety-clack,
Clickety-*clickety*
Clackety
Clack.

David McCord

Night

The night is coming softly, slowly;

Look, it's getting hard to see.

Through the windows,

Through the door,

Pussyfooting

On the floor,

Dragging shadows,

Crawling,

Creeping,

Soon it will be time for sleeping.

Pull down the shades.

Turn on the light.

Let's pretend it isn't night.

Mary Ann Hoberman

When All the World's Asleep

Where do insects go at night,
When all the world's asleep?
Where do bugs and butterflies
and caterpillars creep?

Turtles sleep inside their shells;
The robin has her nest.
Rabbits and the sly old fox
Have holes where they can rest.

Bears can crawl inside a cave;
The lion has his den.
Cows can sleep inside the barn,
And pigs can use their pen.

But where do bugs and butterflies
And caterpillars creep,
When everything is dark outside
And all the world's asleep?

Anita E. Posey

The Chickens

What a fearful battle,
What a dreadful storm!
Five little chickens
Fighting for a worm.

When the worm had vanished
They all said— Peep— and then
The five little chickens
Were all good friends again.

Rose Fyleman

Little Seeds

Little seeds we sow in spring,
Growing while the robins sing,
Give us carrots, peas and beans,
Tomatoes, pumpkins, squash
and greens.

And we pick them,
One and all,
Through the summer,
Through the fall.

Winter comes, then spring, and then
Little seeds we sow again.

Else Holmelund Minarik

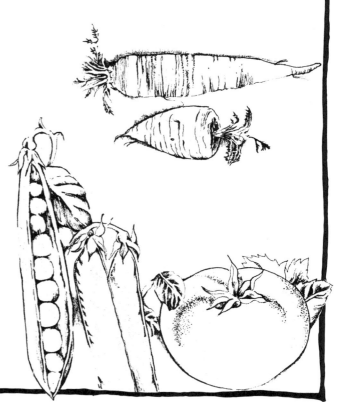

Five Little Chickens

a finger play

Said the first little chicken,
    With a queer little squirm,
"I wish I could find
    A fat little worm."

Said the next little chicken,
    With an odd little shrug,
"I wish I could find
    A fat little bug."

Said the third little chicken,
    With a sharp little squeal,
"I wish I could find
    Some nice yellow meal."

Said the fourth little chicken,
    With a small sigh of grief,
"I wish I could find
    A green little leaf."

Said the fifth little chicken,
    With a faint little moan,
"I wish I could find
    A wee gravel stone."

Said the old mother hen,
    From the green garden patch,
"If you want any breakfast,
    Just come here and scratch."

Dig a Little Hole

a finger play

Dig a little hole, *(Dig.)*

Plant a little seed, *(Drop seed.)*

Pour a little water, *(Pour.)*

Pull a little weed. *(Pull up and throw away.)*

Chase a little bug — *(Make chasing motions with hands.)*

Heigh-ho, there he goes! *(Shade eyes.)*

Give a little sunshine, *(Cup hands, lift to the sun.)*

Grow a little rose. *(Smell flower, smiling.)*

The Little Turtle

There was a little turtle,
   (Make small circle with hands.)
He lived in a box,
   (Make box with both hands.)
He swam in a puddle,
   (Wiggle fingers.)
He climbed on the rocks.
   (Climb fingers of one hand over the other.)
He snapped at a mosquito,
   (Clap hands.)
He snapped at a flea,
   (Clap hands.)
He snapped at a minnow,
   (Clap hands.)
He snapped at me.
   (Point to self.)
He caught the mosquito,
   (Hold hands up, palms facing; quickly bend fingers shut.)
He caught the flea,
   (Repeat.)
He caught the minnow,
   (Repeat.)
But he didn't catch me.
   (Bend fingers only halfway shut and shake head.)

Vachel Lindsay

In the Clear Water

In the clear water
That spurts from the fountain,
One sweet little fish
Suddenly comes up.

Sweet little fish
Won't you come out, please?
Come out and play with me,
We'll go to the garden.

I live in the water,
I cannot come out,
For if I should try
I would surely die.

Sweet little fish
Won't you come out, please?
Come and play with me,
We'll go to the garden.

My mother has warned me . . .
"Don't ever leave,
For if you do,
You will surely die."

Sweet little fish
I should love you so,
Because you obey
And respect your mom.

Entre el agua claro

Entre el agua claro
Que brota en la fuente,
Un lindo pececiso
Sale de repente.

Lindo pececiso
¿No quieres salir
a jugar conmigo?
vamos al jardín.

Yo vivo en el agua
No puedo salir;
Porque si me salgo
Me puedo morir.

Lindo pececiso
¿No quieres salir
a jugar conmigo?
vamos al jardín.

Mi mamá me ha dicho:
No salgas de aquí,
Porque si te sales
te vas a morir.

Lindo pececiso
Yo te debo amar;
Porque a tu mamita
sabes respetar.

If You Ever

If you ever ever ever ever ever
    If you ever ever ever meet a whale
You must never never never never never
    You must never never never touch its tail:
For if you ever ever ever ever ever,
    If you ever ever ever touch its tail,
You will never never never never never,
    You will never never meet another whale.

Frog's Lullaby

Sleep, my pretty polliwog,
Polly wolly wiggle wog

    Polly wiggle waggle wog
    Wiggle waggle woggle wog

Polly wolly wiggle waggle
Wiggle waggle woggle froggle

    Sleep, my little wiggle head,
    In your little water bed.

Sweet dreams, pretty polliwog.
When you wake, you'll be a frog.

Charlotte Pomerantz

31

I'll Tell You a Story

I'll tell you a story

About Jack-a-Nory:

And now my story's begun.

I'll tell you another

About his big brother:

And now my story is done.

The Three Bears

retold by Anne Rockwell

Once upon a time there were three bears who lived together in a house of their own in the woods. One of them was a little wee bear, and one was a middle-sized bear, and the third was a great big bear. They each had a bowl for their porridge—a little bowl for the little wee bear, and a middle-sized bowl for the middle-sized bear, and a great big bowl for the great big bear. And they each had a chair to sit on—a little chair for the little wee bear, and a middle-sized chair for the middle-sized bear, and a great big chair for the great big bear. And they each had a bed to sleep in—a little bed for the little wee bear, and a middle-sized bed for the middle-sized bear, and a great big bed for the great big bear.

One day, after they had made the porridge for their breakfast and poured it into their bowls, they walked out in the woods while the porridge was cooling. A little girl named Goldilocks passed by the house and looked in at the window. And then she looked in at the keyhole, and when she saw that there was no one home, she lifted the latch on the door.

The door was not locked because the bears were good bears who never did anyone any harm and never thought that anyone would harm them. So Goldilocks opened the door and walked in. She was very glad to see the porridge on the table, as she was hungry from walking in the woods, and so she set about helping herself.

First she tasted the porridge of the great big bear, but that was too hot for her. Next she tasted the porridge of the middle-sized bear, but that was too cold for her. And then she tasted the porridge of the little wee bear, and that was neither too hot nor too cold but just right, and she liked it so much that she ate it all up.

Then Goldilocks sat down on the chair of the great big bear, but that was too hard for her. And then she sat down on the chair of the middle-sized bear, and that was too soft for her. And then she sat down on the chair of the little wee bear, and that was neither too hard nor too soft, but just right. So she seated herself in it, and there she sat until she sat the bottom out of the chair and down she came upon the floor.

Then Goldilocks went upstairs to the bedroom where the three bears slept.

And first she lay down upon the bed of the great big bear, but that was too high for her. And next she lay down upon the bed of the middle-sized bear, but that was too low for her. But when she lay down upon the bed of the little wee bear, it was neither too high nor too low, but just right. So she covered herself up comfortably and fell fast asleep.

When the three bears thought their porridge would be cool enough for them to eat, they came home for breakfast. Now Goldilocks had left the spoon of the great big bear standing in the porridge.

"Somebody has been eating my porridge!" said the great big bear in a great, rough gruff voice.

Then the middle-sized bear looked at its porridge and saw the spoon was standing in it, too.

"Somebody has been eating *my* porridge!" said the middle-sized bear in a middle-sized voice.

Then the little wee bear looked at its bowl, and there was the spoon standing in the bowl, but the porridge was all gone.

"Somebody has been eating my porridge and has eaten it all up!" said the little wee bear in a little wee voice.

Upon this, the three bears, seeing that someone had come into their house and eaten up all the little wee bear's breakfast, began to look around them.

Now Goldilocks had not put the cushion straight when she rose from the chair of the great big bear.

"Somebody has been sitting in my chair!" said the great big bear in a great, rough gruff voice.

And Goldilocks had squashed down the soft cushion of the middle-sized bear.

"Somebody has been sitting in my chair!" said the middle-sized bear in a middle-sized voice.

"Somebody has been sitting in my chair, and has sat the bottom through!" said the little wee bear in a little wee voice.

Then the three bears thought that they had better look further in case it was a burglar, so they went upstairs into their bedroom. Now Goldilocks had pulled the pillow of the great big bear out of its place.

"Somebody has been lying in my bed!" said the great big bear in a great, rough gruff voice.

And Goldilocks had pulled the cover of the middle-sized bear out of its place.

"Somebody has been lying in my bed!" said the middle-sized bear in a middle-sized voice.

But when the little wee bear came to look at its bed, there was the pillow in its place. But *upon* the pillow? There was Goldilocks' head, which was not in its place, for she had no business there.

"Somebody has been lying in my bed, and here she is still," said the little wee bear in a little wee voice.

Now Goldilocks had heard in her sleep the great, rough gruff voice of the great big bear, but she was so fast asleep that it was no more to her than the rumbling of distant thunder. And she had heard the middle-sized voice of the middle-sized bear, but it was only as if she had heard someone speaking in a dream. But when she heard the little wee voice of the little wee bear, it was so sharp and so shrill that it woke her up at once.

Up she sat, and when she saw the three bears on one side of the bed, she tumbled out at the other and ran to the window. Now the window was open, for the bears were good, tidy bears who always opened their bedroom window in the morning to let in the fresh air and sunshine. So Goldilocks jumped out through the window and ran away, and the three bears never saw anything more of her.

Chicken Forgets

by Miska Miles

"Chicken," the mother hen said, "I need your help. I want you to go berry hunting. I need a basket of wild blackberries."

"I'd like to go berry hunting," the little chicken said.

"Take this basket and fill it to the top," the mother hen said. "Sometimes you forget things. THIS time, please, please keep your mind on what you are doing. Don't forget."

"I won't forget," the little chicken said. "I'll hunt for wild blackberries."

He started across the meadow. And because he didn't want to forget, he said to himself over and over again, "Get wild blackberries. Get wild blackberries."

All the way to the narrow river he kept saying, "Get wild blackberries."

Then the chicken heard the rusty voice of an old frog.

"What are you saying?" the frog asked.

"Get wild blackberries," the chicken said.

"If you're talking to me, you shouldn't say that," the frog said.

"Oh?" said the chicken. "What SHOULD I say?"

"Get a big green fly," the frog said.

The chicken went on his way. And because he didn't want to forget, he said to himself, "Get a big green fly. Get a big green fly."

All the way to the pasture he said, "Get a big green fly."

At the pasture, a goat pushed his head through the rails of the fence and twitched his beard.

"If you are talking to ME," he said, "you should NOT say, 'Get a green fly.' You should say, 'Get green weeds.' "

"Oh?" said the chicken. And on he went, past the pasture, saying, "Get green weeds. Get green weeds."

A bee buzzed over his head.

"What are you mumbling?" the bee asked.

"I was only saying, 'Get weeds,' " the chicken said.

"I think that's wrong," the bee said. "You should say, 'Get clover blossoms.' "

So the little chicken said, "Get clover blossoms."

He said, "Get clover blossoms" all the way to the edge of the cornfield.

"No, no," said a robin. "Berries are better. Follow me."

So the little chicken ran along the ground, following the robin's shadow, and he came to a beautiful patch of wild blackberries.

The robin flew down and ate until he could eat no more.

And the little chicken filled his basket with beautiful, shining wild blackberries.

He started home. Back he went, through the cornfield and beside the pasture fence by the river.

He ate five berries.

Across the meadow he went.

And he ate three berries.

At home, the mother hen looked at the basket.

"You DIDN'T forget," she said. "You brought home blackberries, and the basket is almost full."

The little chicken said, "It's easy to remember when you really try."

"I'm proud of you," his mother said.

And the little chicken was proud, too.

Will I Have a Friend?

by Miriam Cohen

When Pa was taking Jim to school for the first time, Jim said, "Will I have a friend at school?"

"I think you will," said Pa. And Pa smiled down at him.

In the big schoolroom Pa said, "Good-by." Jim didn't say anything. He didn't want to say good-by.

"Come, Jim," the teacher said. All the boys were making noise. All the girls were laughing. Where was his friend?

The teacher said, "Here is Bill. He is a rocket man."

Bill said "Rrrrrrrr" and he rocketed off.

Anna-Maria walked by. She was pulling a wagon filled with blocks. Jim looked at them. Anna-Maria skipped away.

Jim went over to a big table. There were lumps and humps of gray clay on it. The children were pulling and pinching, poking and patting the clay. They were making snakes, hills, holes and a banana.

Jim reached out and touched the clay. It was cool and wet. When he picked it up, it was heavy. Jim made a man. But he did not know any friend to show him to.

Now it was orange juice and cooky time.

George said, "I want to pass the cookies!"

"Look!" shouted Bill. "I bit the moon!"

"So did I," said Anna-Maria. Jim thought of something to say. He said it to Joseph. But Joseph's mouth was full of cookies. He didn't answer. The pitcher was empty. Juice time was over.

Sara was telling Margaret a secret. Jim looked at them. Where was his friend?

Danny was shouting, "Let's do funny-tummies!" Danny poked out his tummy and bumped Willy's. Willy bumped Sammy's.

When they bumped they laughed and yelled, "Hello, Mr. Funny Tummy!" And Jim laughed too.

The teacher called, "Come to story time!" All the children came running. Jim sat next to Paul. The teacher read them a book about a monkey. Danny jumped up.

"I'm a monkey!" he said. He put his tongue in his lip, and stuck his fingers in his ears. Jim thought he looked just like a monkey.

The teacher said, "It's time for monkeys to rest." They lay down on their mats. It was hard for them to lie still. Jim looked at the ceiling. He scratched his foot. Then he rolled over. Then he rolled back. Someone was looking at him. It was Paul. He had something in his hand. When rest time was over, everyone got up.

"Look what I have," said Paul. He showed Jim a tiny truck. Jim reached out and Paul put it in his hand.

"The doors really work," said Paul.

"I have a gas pump," said Jim. "I'll bring it tomorrow."

Anna-Maria called, "Jim and Paul! Don't you want to play?"

"OK, Jim?" asked Paul.

"OK!" said Jim.

After school, skipping home, Jim said to Pa, "Do you know what? I have a friend at school."

"I thought you would," said Pa. And Pa smiled down at him.

41

Mother, Mother, I Want Another

by Maria Polushkin

It was bedtime in the mouse house. Mrs. Mouse took baby mouse to his room. She helped him put on his pajamas and told him to brush his teeth. She tucked him into his bed and read him a bedtime story. She gave him a bedtime kiss, and then she said "Goodnight." But as she was leaving, baby mouse started to cry. "Why are you crying?" asked Mrs. Mouse.

"I want another, Mother."

"Another mother!" cried Mrs. Mouse. "Where will I find another mother for my baby?"

Mrs. Mouse ran to get Mrs. Duck.

"Please, Mrs. Duck, come to our house and help put baby mouse to bed. Tonight he wants another mother."

Mrs. Duck came and sang a song:

Quack, quack, mousie,
Don't you fret.
I'll bring you worms
Both fat and wet.

But baby mouse said, "Mother, Mother, I want another."

Mrs. Duck went to get Mrs. Frog. Mrs. Frog came and sang:

Croak, croak, mousie,
Close your eyes.
I will bring you
Big fat flies.

But baby mouse said, "Mother, Mother, I want another."

Mrs. Frog went to get Mrs. Pig. Mrs. Pig came and sang a song:

Oink, oink, mousie,
Go to sleep.
I'll bring some carrots
For you to keep.

But baby mouse said, "Mother, Mother, I want another."

Mrs. Pig went to get Mrs. Donkey. Mrs. Donkey came and sang a song:

Hee-haw, mousie,
Hush-a-bye.
I'll sing for you
A lullaby.

But baby mouse had had enough. "NO MORE MOTHERS!" he shouted. "I want another KISS."

"Really?"

"Well, now!"

"Oh?"

"Indeed?"

"I see."

Mrs. Duck kissed baby mouse. Mrs. Frog kissed baby mouse. Mrs. Pig kissed baby mouse. And Mrs. Donkey kissed baby mouse.

Then Mrs. Mouse gave baby mouse a drink of water. She tucked in his blanket. And she gave him a kiss. Baby mouse smiled. "May I have another, Mother?"

"Of course," said Mrs. Mouse, and she leaned over and gave him *another* kiss.

The Gingerbread Man

retold by Anne Rockwell

Once upon a time there was a little old woman and a little old man, and they lived all alone. They were very happy together, but they wanted a child and since they had none, they decided to make one out of gingerbread. So one day the little old woman and the little old man made themselves a little gingerbread man, and they put him in the oven to bake.

When the gingerbread man was done, the little old woman opened the oven door and pulled out the pan.

Out jumped the little gingerbread man— and away he ran. The little old woman and the little old man ran after him as fast as they could, but he just laughed and said,

"Run, run, as fast as you can.
You can't catch me!
I'm the Gingerbread Man!"
And they couldn't catch him.

The gingerbread man ran on and on until he came to a cow. "Stop, little gingerbread man," said the cow. "I want to eat you."

But the gingerbread man said, "I have run away from a little old woman and a little old man, and I can run away from you, too. I can, I can!"

And the cow began to chase the gingerbread man, but the gingerbread man ran faster, and said,

"Run, run, as fast as you can.
You can't catch me!
I'm the Gingerbread Man!"
And the cow couldn't catch him.

The gingerbread man ran on until he came to a horse.

"Please, stop, little gingerbread man," said the horse. "I want to eat you."

And the gingerbread man said, "I have run away from a little old woman, a little old man, and a cow, and I can run away from you, too. I can, I can!"

And the horse began to chase the gingerbread man, but the gingerbread man ran faster and called to the horse,

"Run, run, as fast as you can.
You can't catch me!
I'm the Gingerbread Man!"
And the horse couldn't catch him.

By and by the gingerbread man came to a field full of farmers.

"Stop," said the farmers. "Don't run so fast. We want to eat you."

But the gingerbread man said, "I have run away from a little old woman, a little old man, a cow, and a horse, and I can run away from you, too. I can, I can!"

And the farmers began to chase him, but the gingerbread man ran faster than ever and said,

"Run, run, as fast as you can.
You can't catch me!
I'm the Gingerbread Man!"

And the farmers couldn't catch him.

The gingerbread man ran faster and faster. He ran past a school full of children.

"Stop, little gingerbread man," said the children. "We want to eat you."

But the gingerbread man said, "I have run away from a little old woman, a little old man, a cow, and a horse, a field full of farmers, and I can run away from you, too. I can, I can!"

And the children began to chase him, but the gingerbread man ran faster as he said,

"Run, run, as fast as you can.
You can't catch me!
I'm the Gingerbread Man!"

And the children couldn't catch him.

By this time the gingerbread man was so proud of himself he didn't think anyone could catch him. Pretty soon he saw a fox. The fox looked at him and began to run after him. But the gingerbread man said, "You can't catch me! I have run away from a little old woman, a little old man, a cow, a horse, a field full of farmers, a school full of children, and I can run away from you, too. I can, I can!

"Run, run, as fast as you can.
You can't catch me!
I'm the Gingerbread Man!"

"Oh," said the fox, "I do not want to catch you. I only want to help you run away."

Just then the gingerbread man came to a river. He could not swim across, and he had to keep running.

"Jump on my tail," said the fox. "I will take you across."

So the gingerbread man jumped on the fox's tail, and the fox began to swim across the river. When he had gone a little way, he said to the gingerbread man, "You are too heavy on my tail. Jump on my back."

And the gingerbread man did.

The fox swam a little farther, and then he said, "I am afraid you will get wet on my back. Jump on my shoulder."And the gingerbread man did.

In the middle of the river, the fox said, "Oh, dear, my shoulder is sinking. Jump on my nose, and I can hold you out of the water."

So the little gingerbread man jumped on the fox's nose, and the fox threw back his head and snapped his sharp teeth.

"Oh, dear," said the gingerbread man, "I am a quarter gone!"

Next minute he said, "Now I am half gone!"

And next minute he said, "Oh, my goodness gracious! I am three quarters gone!"

And then the gingerbread man never said anything more at all.

Mr. Floop's Lunch

by Matt Novak

On a day too beautiful to stay inside, Mr. Floop packed a delicious lunch and took it to the park.

When he found a nice spot, he opened his bag and took out a soft, warm roll. Mr. Floop loved rolls.

A bird perched on the bench.

"Would you like a bit of roll?" asked Mr. Floop, and he gave some crumbs to the bird…and to all the other birds. When the roll was gone, the birds flew away.

Mr. Floop reached into his bag again and pulled out a string of juicy sausages. A small dog trotted over to the bench.

"I know what you want," said Mr. Floop, and he gave some sausage to the dog…and to all the other dogs. When the sausages were gone…the dogs ran away.

Mr. Floop took some crunchy peanuts out of the bag. A squirrel crawled down the branch of a tree. Mr. Floop fed a peanut to the squirrel…and to all the other squirrels. When the peanuts were gone…the squirrels ran away.

Mr. Floop took a bottle of milk from his bag and poured himself a nice cool cupful. A tiny kitten jumped onto the bench and purred very loudly. Mr. Floop looked at the kitten, and then he looked all around. There didn't seem to be any others.

48

"Well," he said, "maybe just a little." And he gave some milk to the kitten… and to all the other kittens. When the milk was gone, the kittens ran away.

Mr. Floop sighed. He'd given his bread to the birds, his sausages to the dogs, his peanuts to the squirrels, and his milk to the kittens. He was very hungry.

Mr. Floop was still hungry when a woman came by carrying a picnic basket.

"Excuse me," she said. "May I sit here?"

"Please do," said Mr. Floop.

"Thank you," said the woman. "This is my favorite bench." She sat down next to him.

"Yes, it is nice," said Mr. Floop.

"I come here every day and share my lunch with the animals," she said. "I wonder where they are."

"I don't think they're hungry," said Mr. Floop.

"Really?" said the woman.

"Not anymore," he answered.

Then she saw Mr. Floop's empty bag. She smiled.

"Would you like to share my lunch?" she asked.

"I suppose I could eat a bite or two," Mr. Floop said.

"I don't like to eat alone," the woman said, and she handed Mr. Floop a soft, warm roll.

"Thank you," he said. "I love rolls."

"And I like sharing lunch."

49

The Lion and the Mouse

retold by Anne Rockwell

made to trap him. He roared and roared, and his roars made the leaves on the trees tremble, but still he could not free himself from the net.

Far away the little mouse heard him roar. He hurried to the place where the big lion lay trapped.

"Remember, I promised you I would someday do something good for you," said the little mouse, and he began to nibble on the ropes of the net with his sharp little teeth. He nibbled and nibbled and nibbled some more until there was a big hole in the net.

Then the lion was free, and the lion and the mouse walked away together.

A lion lay sleeping. A little mouse ran across his paw. That tickled the lion and woke him up. He roared and grabbed the little mouse.

"Please," said the little mouse, "do not hurt me. I am sorry I woke you up, but if you do not hurt me, I promise I will do something good for you someday."

The lion laughed. "How silly," he thought. "What could a tiny little mouse do for a big, strong lion like me?" But he let him go.

Soon after, the lion was walking through the forest when suddenly he was caught in a net some hunters had

Angus and the Cat

by Marjorie Flack

Each day as Angus grew older, he grew longer but not much higher. Scottie dogs grow that way.

Now as Angus grew older and longer, he learned MANY THINGS.

He learned it is best to stay in one's own yard.

He learned that frogs can jump but dogs must NOT jump after them.

Angus also learned NOT to lie on the sofa and NOT to take somebody else's food and things like that.

Now there was something outdoors Angus was very curious about but had never learned about, and that was CATS. His leash was always too short.

Then one day what should Angus find indoors lying on the sofa but a strange little CAT!

Angus came closer.

The cat sat up.

Angus came closer.

Up jumped the cat onto the arm of the sofa. Angus came closer and —siss-s-s-s-s-s!!! That little cat boxed Angus's ears! Woo-oo-oof— woo-oo-oof! said Angus.

Up jumped the cat onto the sofa back, up to the mantel, and Angus was not high enough to reach her.

But at lunchtime down she came to try and take Angus's food— though not for long.

Up she jumped onto the table, and Angus was not high enough to reach her.

At nap time there she was sitting in Angus's own special square of sunshine—washing her face— though not for long.

51

Up she jumped onto the window sill, and Angus was not high enough to reach her!

For three whole days Angus was very busy chasing that cat, but she always went up out of reach. On the fourth day he chased her up the stairs, and into the bedroom. But she was completely gone!

Angus looked under the bed. No cat was there.

Angus looked out of the window into his yard, into the next yard, and the next. No cat was in sight.

Angus went down the stairs.

He looked on the sofa. No cat was there. He looked on the mantel. No cat was there. Angus looked on the table and on the window sills. No cat was indoors a-n-y-w-h-e-r-e.

So Angus was all alone. There was no cat to box his ears. There was no cat to take his food. There was no cat to sit in his sunshine. There was no cat to chase away. So Angus had nothing to do!

Angus missed the little cat.

But at lunchtime he heard a noise. *Purrrrr*. There she was again.

And Angus knew and the cat knew that Angus was glad the cat came back!

The Baby Beebee Bird

by Diane Redfield Massie

The animals at the zoo had roared and growled and hissed and meowed all day long. They were very tired.

"It's eight o'clock," yawned the elephant, and he settled down in his big hay bed. "I've eaten 562 peanuts today," he said, but no one heard him. They were all asleep.

The zoo was very still…until… "beebeebobbibobbi beebeebobbibobbi beebeebobbibobbi beebeebobbibobbi…"

"What," said the elephant, "is that?"

"It's the baby beebee bird," said the giraffe. "He's new to the zoo."

"Well, tell him to be quiet," growled the leopard. "I want to sleep."

"beebeebobbibobbi beebeebobbibobbi beebeebobbibobbi beebeebobbibobbi…"

"Be quiet, please," said the giraffe politely.

"But I can't," said the beebee bird. "I'm wide awake. beebeebobbibobbi beebeebobbibobbi beebeebobbibobbi beebeebobbibobbi…"

"Quiet!" roared the lion.

"He's wide awake," explained the giraffe.

53

"Why isn't he tired like the rest of us?" growled the bear.

"Aren't you tired?" asked the giraffe.

"No," said the beebee bird. "I've slept all the day and now it's time for me to sing…beebeebobbibobbi beebee- bobbibobbi beebeebobbibobbi beebeebobbibobbi…"

"Oh, dear," said the elephant, "and I'm so sleepy."

"beebeebobbibobbi beebeebobbibobbi beebeebobbibobbi beebeebobbibobbi…"

"QUIET!!!" shouted all the animals. "WE CAN'T SLEEP!!!"

"beebeebobbibobbi beebeebobbibobbi…" *all night long.*

The sun rose in the morning on a very tired zoo. "What can be the matter?" said the keeper. "The animals must be sick. The elephant is still lying down, the lion is standing on his head, the monkeys won't swing by their tails. Oh, dear me." And he hurried away.

"beebeebobbibobbi," said the beebee bird cheerfully, and he settled down for his morning nap.

The lion whispered to the bear, and the bear nodded to the others. The beebee bird was at last asleep.

"BEEBEEBOBBI," roared the lion.

"BEEBEEBOBBI," trumpeted the elephant.

"BEEBEEBOBBI," growled the bear.

54

"BEEBEEBOBBIBOBBI!!!" sang all the animals together.

"Quiet," said the beebee bird. "Can't you see that I'm sleeping? It's time for my nap."

"BEEBEEBOBBIBOBBI BEEBEE-BOBBIBOBBI!!!" they roared.

The keeper came running with his arms in the air. "SOMETHING IS WRONG!" he said. "SOMETHING IS VERY WRONG WITH THE ANIMALS! WHATEVER SHALL I DO?" And he jumped up and down with alarm.

"BEEBEEBOBBI!!!" sang the animals all day long…

And the baby beebee bird simply couldn't sleep at all.

—The sun went down and the moon came up.—

"Beebeebobbi," whispered the lion, who was too tired to roar.

"Bobbibeebee," sighed the elephant as he closed his eyes.

"Bee…bee…bob…bi…" said a monkey, half to himself.

And then…all was still.

The moon shone down upon a sleeping zoo.

Not an ear or a tail or a whisker moved, and high, high up in the linden tree a tiny bird, inside a leaf, was fast asleep.

And now every day at the zoo you can hear "beebeebobbibobbi beebee-bobbibobbi" in between the lion's roars, but at night there is never a sound. Nighttime is really best for sleeping… especially for very little birds.

Challenge of the Sun and the Wind

a Kenyan folktale

The Sun and the Wind got into an argument one day. They wanted to see who was stronger than the other. They saw a man coming in the street and they each said to the other, "Well, if you think you are stronger than I am, let's see who is going to make that man take off his coat."

So the Sun told the Wind to go ahead and start. The Wind started blowing and blowing and blowing and blowing and blowing and blowing very hard. The man didn't take off the coat.

So the Sun took over and the Sun burnt his rays down and it was so hot. And the man got soooo hot and he said, "I'm soooo hot; let me go and rest under the tree."

So he went under the tree to rest and before he sat down he took off his coat.

The Sun won.

The Three Billy-Goats Gruff

told by P. C. Asbjörnsen

Once upon a time there were three billy-goats, who wanted to go up to the hillside to make themselves fat, and the name of all three was Gruff.

On the way up was a bridge over a mountain stream they had to cross; and under the bridge lived a great ugly Troll, with eyes as big as saucers, and a nose as long as a poker.

The first to cross the bridge was the youngest billy-goat Gruff.

"*Trip, trap; trip, trap!*" went the bridge.

"*Who's that* tripping over my bridge?" roared the Troll.

"Oh! It is only I, the tiniest billy-goat Gruff; and I'm going up to the hillside to make myself fat," said the billy-goat with such a small voice.

"Well, I'm coming to gobble you up," said the Troll.

"Oh, no! Please don't gobble me up. I'm too little, that I am," said the billy-goat. "Wait a bit till the second billy-goat Gruff comes. He's much bigger."

"Well! Be off with you," said the Troll.

A little while later the second billy-goat Gruff came to cross the bridge.

"*Trip, trap! Trip, trap! Trip, trap!*" went the bridge.

"*Who's that* tripping over my bridge?" roared the Troll.

"Oh! It's I, the second billy-goat Gruff, and I'm going up to the hillside to make myself fat," said the billy-goat, who hadn't such a small voice.

"Well, I'm coming to gobble you up," said the Troll.

"Oh, no! Please don't gobble me up. Wait a little till the big billy-goat Gruff comes. He's much bigger."

"Very well! Be off with you," said the Troll.

But just then up came the big billy-goat Gruff.

"*Trip, trap! Trip, trap! Trip, trap!*" went the bridge, for the billy-goat was so heavy that the bridge creaked and groaned under him.

"*Who's that* tramping over my bridge?" roared the Troll.

"*It's I! The big billy-goat Gruff,*" said the billy-goat, who had an ugly, hoarse voice of his own.

"Well, I'm coming to gobble you up," roared the Troll.

"*Well, come along!*
I've got two spears,
And I'll poke your nose
and pierce your ears;
I've got besides two curling stones,
And I'll bruise your body
and rattle your bones."

That was what the big billy-goat said; and then he flew at the Troll and tossed him into the water. And the third billy-goat Gruff went up to the hillside. There the billy-goats got so fat they were scarcely able to walk home again; and if the fat hasn't fallen off them, why they're still fat, and so:

Snip, snap, snout,
This tale's told out.

Coyote and Turtle

a Native American folktale
retold by Joe Hayes

Did you know that turtles are very brave animals? If you stop to think, you'll see they are. They never run away — not even from their fiercest enemies. And they certainly aren't afraid of Coyote.

One fine day in spring the turtles all decided to leave their home in the river and hunt for tender green cactus shoots. They all moved slowly up the river bank and out onto the desert, but Little Turtle, the youngest of the clan, moved the slowest of all.

Little Turtle had never been out of the river before and this new world was fascinating to him. He stopped to investigate each colorful rock or bush or clump of grass. His mother kept calling for him to hurry and catch up.

Then Little Turtle saw a patch of blue flowers. He wandered over to see them more closely, and when he looked up he realized that he was all alone.

Now, as I said, turtles are very brave, but this turtle was so young and this place was so strange that he began to cry — "*hoo-hoo-hoo*" — and turned to go home.

Little Turtle started back toward the river sobbing softly to himself, and who should happen by but Coyote. Coyote sat down and cocked his ear toward Little Turtle. Finally Coyote said, "Little Turtle, what a fine song you're singing!"

"I'm not singing," Little Turtle pouted. "I'm crying! Don't you know the difference between singing and crying?"

Coyote paid no attention. "Yes," he went on, "I know good music when I hear it. That is a fine song. Sing it a little louder for me."

"I told you I'm not singing. *I'm crying!*"

Now Coyote grew impatient. "Little Turtle, if you don't sing me your song good and loud, I'll swallow you whole."

That would be enough to frighten any other animal Little Turtle's size, but Little Turtle's mother had told him about Coyote. He knew what to do. He told Coyote, "Go on—swallow me. I'll bounce around in your stomach like a stone and kill you."

Coyote reached out a paw and touched Little Turtle's shell. It was hard as stone.

"Well, then," Coyote said, "I'll jump on you with all four feet and crush you!"

"Go ahead and try it. My shell is strong. It won't hurt me a bit. My mother told me so."

"What if I throw you against a rock?"

"The rock will break," Little Turtle said. "I won't feel a thing. My mother told me only one thing can hurt me."

Now Coyote changed his tone. "Really?" he praised. "How strong you are! Only one thing can hurt you? Let me guess what it is: It must be Mountain Lion's sharp claws."

62

Little Turtle laughed, "Mountain Lion's claws will break on my shell."

"Then maybe it's Bear's powerful jaws?"

"Bear might as well try to crush a rock with his jaws. My shell will be harder."

"I give up, Little Turtle. Tell me what it is."

"My mother said that nothing can hurt me but the cold water of the river." Little Turtle shivered. "Oouuu! I hate cold water!"

Now Coyote laughed. "You foolish turtle. Since you hate water so much, that's just where I'll throw you!" And he picked Little Turtle up in his mouth and ran to the river and threw him into the water.

Little Turtle poked his head out of the water laughing. "Thank you, Coyote," he called out. "The river is where I live. You saved me a long walk back home." And Little Turtle swam away.

Coyote was so angry that he started to cry—"*Howw-ow-ow-ow…*"

A raven in a nearby tree heard Coyote and called down to him, "*Caw!* Coyote, what a beautiful song you're singing!! *Caw!*"

"Stupid bird!" Coyote screamed, "don't you know the difference between singing and crying?"

Franklin in the Dark

by Paulette Bourgeois

Franklin could slide down a river-bank all by himself. He could count forwards and backwards. He could even zip zippers and button buttons. But Franklin was afraid of small, dark places and that was a problem because Franklin was a turtle. He was afraid of crawling into his small, dark shell. And so, Franklin the turtle dragged his shell behind him.

Every night, Franklin's mother would take a flashlight and shine it into his shell.

"See," she would say, "there's nothing to be afraid of."

She always said that. She wasn't afraid of anything. But Franklin was sure that creepy things, slippery things, and monsters lived inside his small, dark shell.

So Franklin went looking for help. He walked until he met a duck.

"Excuse me, Duck. I'm afraid of small, dark places and I can't crawl inside my shell. Can you help me?"

"Maybe," quacked the duck. "You see, I'm afraid of very deep water. Sometimes, when nobody is watching, I wear water wings. Would my water wings help you?"

"No," said Franklin. "I'm not afraid of water."

So Franklin walked and walked until he met a lion.

cuse me, Lion. I'm afraid of small, places and I can't crawl inside my l. Can you help me?"

"Maybe," roared the lion. "You see, I'm afraid of great, loud noises. Sometimes, when nobody is looking, I wear earmuffs. Would my earmuffs help you?"

"No," said Franklin. "I'm not afraid of great, loud noises."

So Franklin walked and walked and walked until he met a bird.

"Excuse me, Bird. I'm afraid of small, dark places and I can't crawl inside my shell. Can you help me?"

"Maybe," chirped the bird.

"I'm afraid of flying so high that I get dizzy and fall to the ground. Sometimes, when nobody is looking, I pull my parachute. Would my parachute help you?"

"No," said Franklin. "I'm not afraid of flying high and getting dizzy."

So Franklin walked and walked and walked and walked until he met a polar bear.

"Excuse me, Polar Bear. I'm afraid of small, dark places and I can't crawl inside my shell. Can you help me?"

"Maybe," growled the bear. "You see, I'm afraid of freezing on icy, cold nights. Sometimes, when nobody is looking, I wear my snowsuit to bed. Would my snowsuit help you?"

"No," said Franklin. "I'm not afraid of freezing on icy, cold nights."

Franklin was tired and hungry. He walked and walked and walked until he met his mother.

"Oh, Franklin. I was so afraid you ~~re lost."

~~ou were afraid? I didn't know ~~rs were ever afraid," said ~~.

~~did you find some help?" she

~~a duck who was afraid of

~~said.

~~on who was afraid of

~~said.

~~rd who was ~~lar bear who

"Oh," she said. "They were all afraid of something."

"Hmmmm," said Franklin.

It was getting late. Franklin was very tired and very hungry. They walked and walked until they were home.

Franklin's mother gave him a cold supper and a warm hug. And then she sent him off to bed.

"Goodnight, dear," she said.

Well, Franklin knew what he had to do. He crawled right inside his small, dark shell. He was sure he saw creepy things, slippery things, and a monster. But he said a brave "Goodnight."

And then, when nobody was looking, Franklin the turtle turned on his night light.

The Turnip

by Alexei Tolstoy

Once upon a time an old man planted a little turnip and said:
"Grow, grow, little turnip, grow sweet! Grow, grow, little turnip,
grow strong!"

And the turnip grew up sweet and strong and big and enormous.

Then, one day, the old man went to pull it up. He pulled and
pulled again, but he could not pull it up.

He called the old woman.

    The old woman pulled the old man,
    The old man pulled the turnip.

And they pulled and pulled again, but they could not pull it up.
So the old woman called her granddaughter.

    The granddaughter pulled the old woman,
    The old woman pulled the old man,
    The old man pulled the turnip.

And they pulled and pulled again, but they could not pull it up.
The granddaughter called the black dog.

    The black dog pulled the granddaughter,
    The granddaughter pulled the old woman,
    The old woman pulled the old man,
    The old man pulled the turnip.

And they pulled and pulled again, but they could not pull it up.

The black dog called the cat.

    The cat pulled the dog,

    The dog pulled the granddaughter,

    The granddaughter pulled the old woman,

    The old woman pulled the old man,

    The old man pulled the turnip.

And they pulled and pulled again, but still they could not pull it up.

    The cat called the mouse.

    The mouse pulled the cat,

    The cat pulled the dog,

    The dog pulled the granddaughter,

    The granddaughter pulled the old woman,

    The old woman pulled the old man,

    The old man pulled the turnip.

And they pulled and pulled again, and up came the turnip at last.

The Seashore Noisy Book

by Margaret Wise Brown

Muffin was a little dog with sharp ears. There was nothing he didn't hear. He could even hear the rain falling. Muffin had heard the trucks roaring through the city and the birds whistling in the country. He thought he had heard everything. But he had never heard the Sea.

Then one day Muffin went to the Sea on a big sailboat. *Ho! Ho!* said the Captain of the boat. *We'll make a little sailor out of Muffin.* Muffin's nose tasted salty when he licked it. All around him was the Sea. Wherever he looked as far as he could see there was cold water and a big sky.

Muffin could taste the Sea.
Muffin could see the Sea.
Muffin could feel the Sea.
And he could smell the Sea.
But could Muffin hear the Sea?

Scree Scree Scree. What was that?
White birds flying in the air.
And way off across the water he heard:
Putt Putt putt putt putt.
What was that?
Then a big Ocean Liner went by and blew all its whistles.
How was that?
And a sailboat sailed by.
But could Muffin hear that?

Then slowly a gray wetness came in the air and Muffin couldn't see very far.
What was that grayness?
Far off in the fog Muffin could hear:
Whoooo Whoooo Whoooo Whoooo.
What was that?
And he could hear:
lapping slapping slap lap lap
against the side of the boat.
What was that?

Then suddenly very close on the other side of the boat he heard:
DONG DONG ding DONG DONG.
And from a nearby island he heard:
Baaaa Baa Baaa.
How was that?
He heard: *Toot Toot Toot Toot.*
What was that?
And he heard a foghorn.
What was that?
And then he heard a flutter of little birds' wings:
sssswishsh-shshshshshshsh.
For when the big noises stop you can hear the little noises.

When the fog was gone and the sun was shining down on the Sea, Muffin went ashore and walked along the beach. First he found a jellyfish lying in the sand.
Could Muffin hear that?

Then he met a snail sliding down a rock.
Could Muffin hear that?
And in a pool under a rock, Muffin found a starfish.
Could Muffin hear that?

Then Muffin found a big Sea Shell. He sniffed all around it. He pushed it with his paw. Then he poked his nose inside the shell. And that was when he heard the noise. What was that soft low noise? It was the sound of the Sea.

Muffin was so busy listening to the noise in the Sea Shell he did not hear the great scuttling crab coming down the beach. Then the crab scuttled up and nearly pinched Muffin's little foot. But Muffin grabbed the old crab by the back and threw him in the Sea.

Then Muffin took a big drink of Sea Water. But he didn't like it. Why was that?

So he walked along in the warm soft sand. And he saw more crabs and pink shells and white shells and jellyfish and an old brown bottle.

At sundown Muffin heard the dinner bell. So he went back on the boat and they had crab soup for supper. Then it was night.

It was night and Muffin didn't hear a thing but the gentle lapping of waves around the boat. The moon and the stars shone down on the Sea. And you could see their lights on the waters. But could Muffin hear that?

The fish swam slowly about the Sea. But could Muffin hear that? And lobsters crawled into lobster pots down in the depths of the Sea. But could Muffin hear that? And a giant shark swam round and round. But could Muffin hear that? And a swordfish. But could Muffin hear that? And some little tiny fish. But could Muffin hear that? And all around under the boat were starfish and barnacles and flounders and periwinkles and whales. But could Muffin hear that?

Then in the morning they went fishing.
Flip flop the Captain caught a fish.
Flip flop flip flop it jumped on the bottom of the boat.
It was a mackerel!
Flip flop flip flop Muffin caught a fish.
Flip flop flip flop it jumped on the bottom of the boat.
It was a flounder!
Flip flop flip flop the Captain caught another fish.
It was a codfish!

Then all of a sudden there was a BIG SPLASHING in the water near the boat.
What could it be?
It was not a whale.
Was it the sun falling out of the sky? *NO*
Was it a walrus blowing through his whiskers? *NO*
Was it a sea horse galloping? *NO*
Was it a little shrimp? *NO*
What do you think it was?

It was Muffin. Swimming and splashing in the Sea. *Ho! Ho!* said the Captain as he pulled Muffin out of the water. *I think I've caught a dogfish this time.*

Sing a Song of Sixpence

Sing a song of sixpence,
A pocket full of rye;
Four-and-twenty blackbirds
Baked in a pie!

When the pie was opened,
The birds began to sing;
Wasn't that a dainty dish
To set before the king?

Barnacle Bill

by Phyllis Weikart

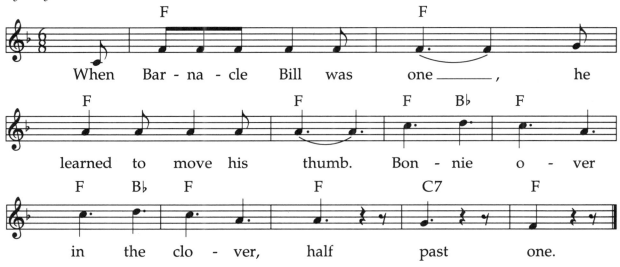

When Barnacle Bill was one _____, he
learned to move his thumb. Bon - nie o - ver
in the clo - ver, half past one.

When Barnacle Bill was two,
he learned to pat his shoe…

When Barnacle Bill was three,
he learned to pat his knee…

When Barnacle Bill was four,
he learned to pat the floor…

When Barnacle Bill was five,
he learned to pat his thigh…

Mary Wore Her Red Dress

F   B♭   F   C7   F   B♭

Ma - ry wore her red dress, Red dress, red dress,

F   B♭   F   C7   F

Ma - ry wore her red dress All day long.

Loop de Loo

Here we go loop de loo, Here we go loop de la, Here we go loop de loo, all on a Sat-ur-day night. I put my right hand in, I put my right hand out, I give my right hand a shake, shake, shake and turn ⎯ my bo-dy a-bout.

I put my left hand in…*etc.*
I put my right foot in…*etc.*
I put my whole self in…*etc.*

What Shall We Do?

Game Song

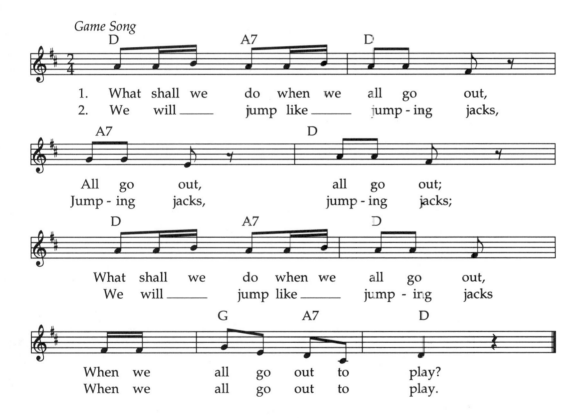

1. What shall we do when we all go out,
2. We will _____ jump like _____ jump - ing jacks,

All go out, all go out;
Jump - ing jacks, jump - ing jacks;

What shall we do when we all go out,
We will _____ jump like _____ jump - ing jacks

When we all go out to play?
When we all go out to play.

We will play a game of tag ...*etc.*
We will climb the jungle gym ...*etc.*

The Bear Went Over the Mountain

The bear went o-ver the moun-tain, The bear went o-ver the moun-tain, The bear went o-ver the moun-tain, To see what he could see. _____ To see what he could see, _____ To see what he could see _____ The oth-er side of the moun-tain, The oth-er side of the moun-tain, The oth-er side of the moun-tain Was all _ that he _ could see. _____

The Mulberry Bush

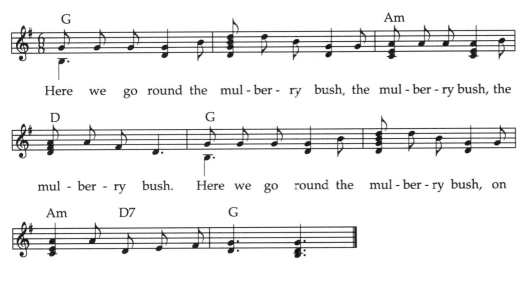

Here we go round the mul-ber-ry bush, the mul-ber-ry bush, the

mul-ber-ry bush. Here we go round the mul-ber-ry bush, on

a cold and fros-ty morn-ing.

This is the way we wash our clothes, ...
So early Monday morning!

This is the way we iron our clothes, ...
So early Tuesday morning!

This is the way we scrub our floors, ...
So early Wednesday morning!

This is the way we mend our clothes, ...
So early Thursday morning!

This is the way we sweep our floors, ...
So early Friday morning!

This is the way we bake our bread, ...
So early Saturday morning!

This is the way we go for a walk, ...
So early Sunday morning!

Did You Ever See a Lassie?

Did you ev - er see a lass - ie, a lass - ie, a lass - ie, Did you ev - er see a lass - ie go this way and that? Go this way and that way, And this way and that way, Did you ev - er see a lass - ie Go this way and that?

Who's That Tapping at the Window?

Who's that tap-ping at the win-dow? Who's that knock-ing at the door?

Mam - my tap-ping at the win-dow, Pap-py knock-ing at the door.

Roll Over

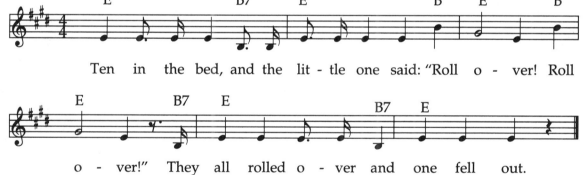

Ten in the bed, and the lit-tle one said: "Roll o - ver! Roll

o - ver!" They all rolled o - ver and one fell out.

Nine in the bed,...*etc.*
Eight in the bed,...*etc.*
Seven in the bed,...*etc.*
Six in the bed,...*etc.*
Five in the bed,...*etc.*
Four in the bed,...*etc.*
Three in the bed,...*etc.*
Two in the bed,...*etc.*
One in the bed, and the little one said:
(*Spoken*) "Alone at last!"

Frère Jacques

(French)

French Traditional Round

Frè - re Jac - ques, Frè - re Jac - ques, Dor - mez vous? Dor - mez vous?

Son - nez les ma - tin - es, Son - nez les ma - tin - es, Din, dan, don, Din, dan, don.

Are you sleeping, are you sleeping,
Brother John, Brother John?
Morning bells are ringing,
Morning bells are ringing,
Ding, ding, dong; ding, ding, dong.

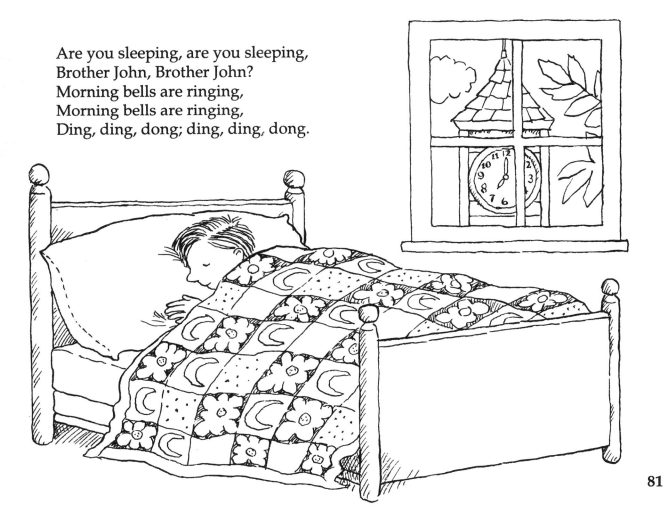

The People in a Family

by Bryan Fitzgerald

The peo-ple in a fam'-ly are diff'-rent as can be.

Some have man-y broth-ers or sis-ters two or three.

Some have a Mom or Dad, Grand-mas, Grand-pas, too. Or

May-be just a ba-by or dog to play with you.

What's your fam'-ly size? Should there be a rule?

Must there be a Mom and Dad, two kids who go to school?

Count the ones you love to find your fam'-ly size.

Know-ing all your rel-a-tives keeps strong your fam'-ly ties.

The Muffin Man

Do you know the muf-fin man, the muf-fin man, the
muf-fin man? Do you know the muf-fin man who
lives in Dru-ry Lane?

Yes, I know the muffin man,
The muffin man, the muffin man.
Yes, I know the muffin man,
Who lives in Drury Lane.

Little Sally Walker

Spirited

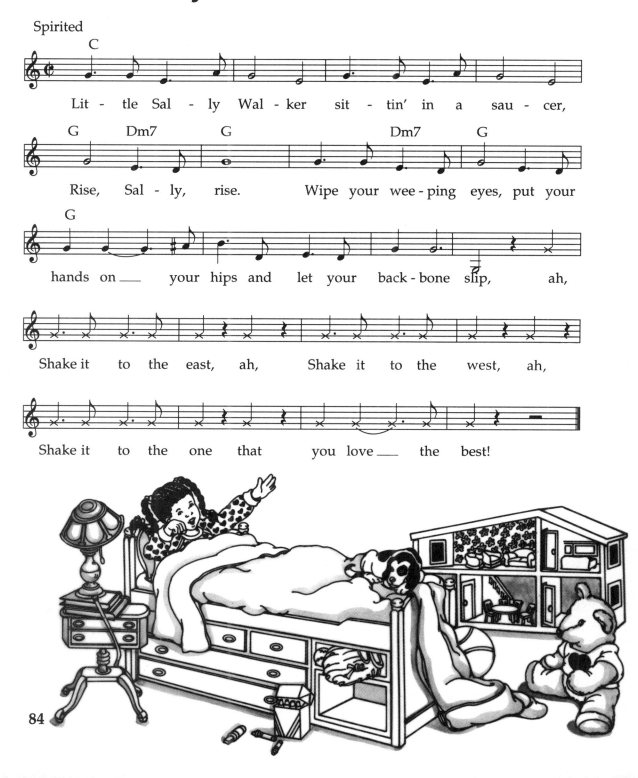

Lit - tle Sal - ly Wal - ker sit - tin' in a sau - cer,

Rise, Sal - ly, rise. Wipe your wee - ping eyes, put your

hands on ___ your hips and let your back - bone slip, ah,

Shake it to the east, ah, Shake it to the west, ah,

Shake it to the one that you love ___ the best!

Old MacDonald Had a Farm

C7

Old Mac - Don - ald had a farm, E - I - E - I - O. And

on that farm he had some chicks, E - I - E - I - O. With a

chick - chick here, and a chick - chick there, Here a chick, there a chick,

ev -'rywhere a chick - chick. Old Mac-Don-ald had a farm, E - I - E - I - O.

Old MacDonald had a farm,
E-I-E-I-O
And on that farm he had some ducks,
E-I-E-I-O
With a quack-quack here,
And a quack-quack there,
Here a quack, there a quack,
Ev-'ry-where a quack-quack,
Chick-chick here,
Chick-chick there,
Here a chick, there a chick,
Ev-'ry-where a chick-chick,
Old MacDonald had a farm,
E-I-E-I-O

Bought Me a Cat

Fast ♩ = 108

1. Bought me a cat, the cat pleased me, Fed my cat un-der yon-ders tree,
Cat went fid - dle - i - fee, fid - dle - i - fee.

2. Bought me a hen, the hen pleased me, Fed my hen un-der yon-ders tree,
Hen went chip - sy chop - sy, Cat went fid - dle - i - fee, fid - dle - i - fee.

3. Bought me a duck, the duck pleased me, Fed my duck un-der yon-ders tree.
Duck went slish - y slosh - y.
Hen went chip - sy chop - sy, Cat went fid - dle - i - fee, fid - dle - i - fee.

Bought me a goose,... Goose went qua,...
Bought me a dog,... Dog went boo,...
Bought me a sheep,... Sheep went baa,...
Bought me a cow,... Cow went moo,...
Bought me a horse,... Horse went neigh,...

Eency Weency Spider

The een-cy ween-cy spi-der went up the wa-ter spout;_____ Down came the rain and washed the spi-der out;_____ Out came the sun and dried up all the rain, And the een-cy ween-cy spi-der went up the spout a-gain._____

Bingo

Gaily

There was a farm-er had a dog, And Bin-go was his name, O! B - I - N - G - O, B - I - N - G - O, B - I - N - G - O, and Bin-go was his name, O!

The Wind Blow East

Oh, the wind blow east, The wind blow west,

The wind blow the *Sun - shine* Right down in town.

Oh, the wind blow the *Sun - shine* Right down in town,

Oh, the wind blow the *Sun - shine* Right down in town.

The Bus Song

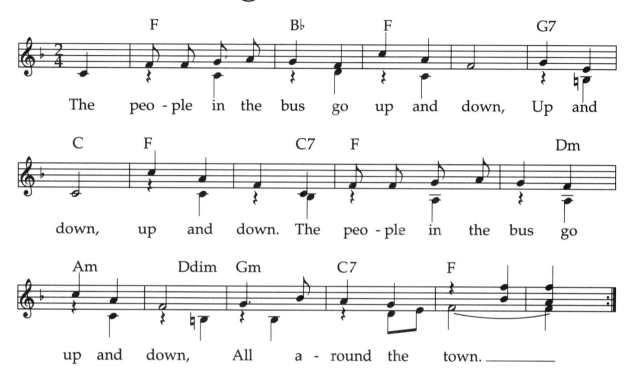

The peo-ple in the bus go up and down, Up and
down, up and down. The peo-ple in the bus go
up and down, All a-round the town. _____

The wiper on the bus goes "Swish, swish,
swish," ... *etc.*
The brake on the bus goes "Roomp, roomp,
roomp," ... *etc.*
The money on the bus goes "Clink, clink,
clink," ... *etc.*

The Allee-Allee O

Oh, the big ship's a - sail - ing through the Al - lee - al - lee
O, the Al - lee - al - lee O, the Al - lee - al - lee
O! Oh, the big ship's a - sail - ing through the Al - lee - al - lee
O! Hi! Ding - dong - day! _____

Riding in My Car

by Woody Guthrie

1. Take you rid - ing in my car, car,
2. En - gine it goes brrm, brrm,

Take you rid - ing in my car, car, Take you rid - ing in my
En - gine it goes brrm, brrm, En - gine it goes

car, car,
brrm, brrm,
I'll take you rid - ing in my car.

Twinkle, Twinkle, Little Star

Gently

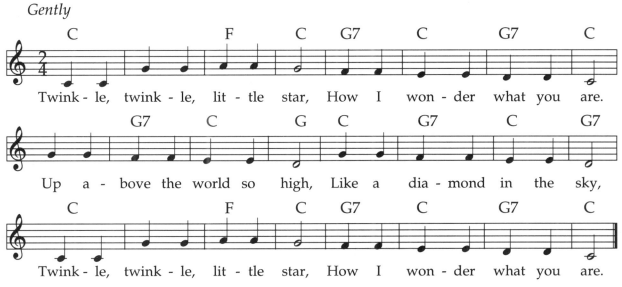

Twink - le, twink - le, lit - tle star, How I won - der what you are.

Up a - bove the world so high, Like a dia - mond in the sky,

Twink - le, twink - le, lit - tle star, How I won - der what you are.

Five Little Frogs

Five green and speck - led frogs sat on a speck - led log,

Eat - ing some most de - li - cious bugs. *(yum, yum)*

One jumped in - to the pool, where it was nice and cool,

Then there were four green speck - led frogs. *(glub, glub)*

Four green and speckled frogs,…*etc.*
Three green and speckled frogs,…*etc.*
Two green and speckled frogs,…*etc.*
One green and speckled frog,…*etc.*
No green and speckled frogs,…*(boo hoo)*